Montana

A ★ SCENIC ★ TREASURE

PHOTOGRAPHY BY
JOHN LAMBING AND WAYNE MUMFORD

Farcountry
PRESS

FRONT COVER: A meadow of purple onion surrounds a pond reflecting Piegan Mountain in Glacier National Park. JOHN LAMBING

TITLE PAGE: A clear winter day in the Mission Mountains near Ronan. WAYNE MUMFORD

COPYRIGHT PAGE: Goat Flat, a glacial cirque, stands at an elevation of 9,200 feet in the Anaconda-Pintler Wilderness. WAYNE MUMFORD

BACK COVER: A salmon-colored sky reflected in the placid surface of DePuy Spring Creek near Livingston. WAYNE MUMFORD

ISBN: 1-56037-262-1

© 2003 Farcountry Press

Photography © John Lambing, Wayne Mumford

Our bookstore appears online at www.montanamagazine.com

Created, designed, and published in the USA.
Printed in Korea.

Little Lake tucked between Homer Youngs Peak and the Continental Divide in the Beaverhead National Forest. JOHN LAMBING

For me, photography is an excuse to explore. I have always been driven to search for hidden places that the crowds have missed. When reading historical accounts of the early explorers, I conjure up mental visions of the stunning scenes they encountered. These visions instill a strong desire to seek out the remaining remnants of those vast landscapes in an attempt to see what they saw. Along the way, I often stumble across many other interesting geologic or cultural features—nice bonuses just for being "out there." With a lot of planning and persistence, I have been rewarded with many magical moments. Although I have had a number of heart-pounding encounters while hiking through rattlesnake or grizzly country in the dim pre-dawn light, being in the right location at the right time is the thrill of the chase.

There is something relaxing and peaceful about settling into a scene represented by a photograph. But as most outdoor recreationists know, a photo can never capture the full sensation of actually being there. The initial glimpse of a breathtaking scene, coupled with the surrounding sounds and smells, merge into an experience that can't be adequately described with either words or pictures. But when you feel it, you know it. So I am determined to experience as many places as I can, fully realizing that I can only scratch the surface of the endless areas to explore in Montana. Living in the midst of incredible natural beauty and being able to fulfill my desire to explore and photograph is a dream come true. And that probably sums it up best—I am living my dream. No one can ask for more than that.

I hope you enjoy the photos and someday have the chance to search for your own magical moments in Montana. Whether you capture them on film, or burn them in your memory, they are always worth the effort.

J.L.

My first trip to Montana was as a seven year old. Everything was big—really big. The sledding hill near our home in Whitefish was enormous, the not-so-big Whitefish River was in fact quite big, and the huckleberries, of course, were huge. Like oversized gophers, we built tunnels through mountains of snow in our backyard. Then we moved.

I did not return until my mid-teens, at which time we crossed the state on a family trip. Already hooked on the early history of the fur men and native peoples on the upper Missouri, I had been reading Vardis Fischer's, *Mountain Man*. By virtue of proximity, the places in the book came to life: the Crazy Mountains, the Missouri and Yellowstone Rivers, and the Absarokas—places that Jeremiah Johnson, the main character in the book, had been. It was here, too, that Johnson, whose encounters with the native population were usually less than amiable, travelled territory claimed by the Crow and the Blackfeet.

I knew that I would return to the state someday. In the interim I read more about the area's history; I read *The Journals of Lewis and Clark* and stories about David Thompson and the traders, trappers, and natives up and down the Clark Fork and the Missouri and Yellowstone Rivers. I felt the tug of these places, and Montana became a magnet that pulled me back. That was more than twenty years ago, and today Montana still holds me fast.

Before picking up a camera, my background was in art—drawing and painting both animals and landscapes. I did not seriously consider a camera as a tool for artistic expression until I moved to Montana.

As a photographer, one is seemingly cutting slices out of time, freezing an instant out of eternity and, for a short time, putting it on display. Montana is full of variety; the land, the weather, and the people all combine to challenge a person trying to share it within the context of a photograph. Near Libby or Glacier National Park one can find a

The Dearborn River weaves through rugged, mountainous terrain in the west-central part of the state. WAYNE MUMFORD

coastal environment similar to that of the Pacific Northwest; travel across the state to Makoshika State Park and you can experience a desert reminiscent of the Southwest. Montana weather is legendary for its ability to change rapidly at any given time of the year. The people, too, are as rich and varied in their lifestyles and history as the land and weather. For me, photography in this environment

is never perfected. It has become an audacious endeavor of combining the inhabitant, history, and environment all into one plane of view. Like a little speed bump in time—a moment captured before it races away into the next instant.

W.M.

ABOVE: A short-eared owl shows off its classic stripes and smoky eyes.
WAYNE MUMFORD

LEFT: Lunch Creek cascades off a cliff near Going-to-the-Sun Road
in Glacier National Park. WAYNE MUMFORD

LEFT: The 18,540-acre National Bison Range near Moiese protects about 400 bison, as well as mule and white-tailed deer, bighorn sheep, and antelope. WAYNE MUMFORD

BELOW: Bright red, historic "Jammer" buses offer tours of Glacier National Park. WAYNE MUMFORD

FACING PAGE: Completed in 1914, St. Helena Cathedral in the capital city is a replica of the Votive Church in Vienna, Austria. JOHN LAMBING

ABOVE: Pintler Falls splashes through the Beaverhead National Forest near Wisdom.
JOHN LAMBING

LEFT: Lush and healthy forest understory along McDonald Creek in Glacier National Park.
WAYNE MUMFORD

ABOVE: Wild horses aren't the only inhabitants of Wild Horse Island State Park; some bighorn sheep live there, too. WAYNE MUMFORD

FACING PAGE: Trapper Peak rises to a perfect point in the Bitterroot National Forest. JOHN LAMBING

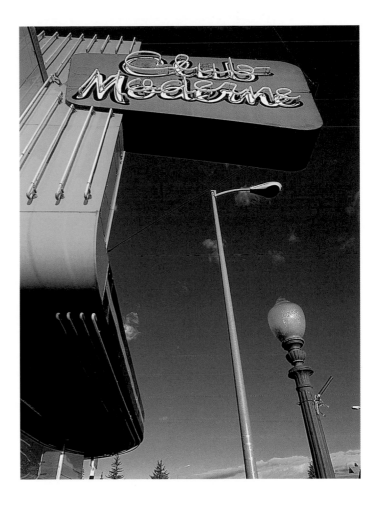

ABOVE: A unique Anaconda nightspot, Club Moderne. WAYNE MUMFORD

LEFT: Big Hole River in the southwestern part of the state is a popular fishing destination. JOHN LAMBING

PRECEDING PAGES: The endless view from Judith Peak near Lewistown. WAYNE MUMFORD

ABOVE: A Glacier National Park mountain goat comes around the bend for a better view.
WAYNE MUMFORD

FACING PAGE: Skalkaho Falls roars down the Sapphire Mountains near Hamilton.
JOHN LAMBING

ABOVE: During the spring and summer months, sailboats can often be seen gliding on the waters of Canyon Ferry Lake near Helena. WAYNE MUMFORD

LEFT: Frozen in place at Quake Lake; this lake was created by a landslide that dammed the Madison River after a 1959 earthquake. WAYNE MUMFORD

ABOVE: A sharp-tailed grouse performs his courting dance. John Lambing

RIGHT: This region in the shadow of the Bears Paw Mountains was the site of a major battle between the U.S. Army and Nez Perce tribesmen in 1877. Wayne Mumford

ABOVE: Volcanic cliffs reflected in the Missouri River near Craig. JOHN LAMBING

FACING PAGE: Winter snow blankets the Pintler Range near Wise River. WAYNE MUMFORD

Above: Mountain bluebirds reside in conifer forests and nest boxes throughout the western part of the state. WAYNE MUMFORD

Right: Storm clouds gather over the wild and scenic Missouri River. JOHN LAMBING

ABOVE: Morning light blazes on a wheat field near Chester. JOHN LAMBING

LEFT: Snow sticks around much of the year atop the high peaks surrounding Lake McDonald in Glacier National Park. WAYNE MUMFORD

ABOVE: Rendezvous encampment on the North Fork of the Flathead River.
WAYNE MUMFORD

FACING PAGE: Alberton Gorge on the Clark Fork is famous for its beautiful alpine scenery and tumbling rapids. JOHN LAMBING

ABOVE: Old and newer sections of the Old Territorial Prison in Deer Lodge; the prison operated from 1871 to 1979. WAYNE MUMFORD

RIGHT: Golden aspen thrives below Sawtooth Mountain in the Snowcrest Range. JOHN LAMBING

Above: Bull-riding at an Augusta rodeo. Wayne Mumford

Left: Some of the tallest mountains in the state, the Beartooth Mountains straddle the Montana/Wyoming border near Yellowstone National Park. John Lambing

ABOVE: A natural route through the tall mountains of northwestern Montana, Marias Pass was used by the Great Northern Railroad as the path for the first rail line to extend across the upper Northwest. WAYNE MUMFORD

FACING PAGE: Falls Creek spills over a dropoff near the confluence of Falls Creek and the Dearborn River. JOHN LAMBING

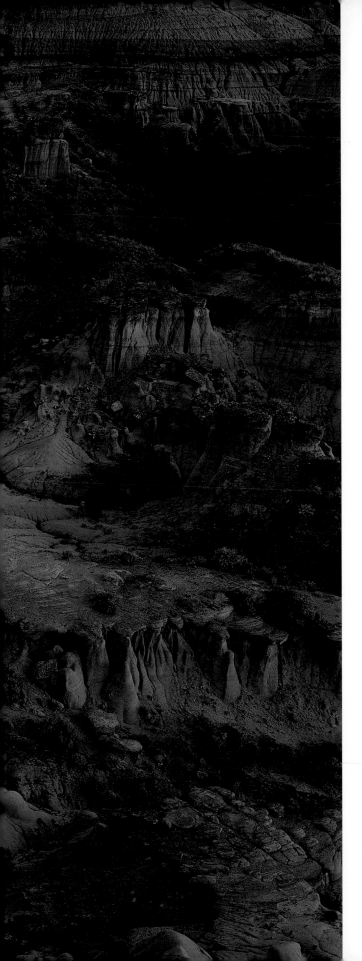

ABOVE: Scatterings of lupine in a meadow near Red Lodge. WAYNE MUMFORD

LEFT: Home to bizarre and whimsical badlands formations, Makoshika State Park can be found near Glendive among the dry and rugged foothills of the eastern part of the state. WAYNE MUMFORD

ABOVE: A lucky observer may spot a moose in mountain meadows or marshy areas in the western third of the state. JOHN LAMBING

FACING PAGE: Full moon sets over an old homestead near Avon. JOHN LAMBING

ABOVE: Colorful wildflowers announce spring in Glacier National Park.
WAYNE MUMFORD

LEFT: A dusting of snow on Mount Cannon in Glacier National Park.
WAYNE MUMFORD

ABOVE: A dazzling Glacier National Park sight, Bird Woman Falls is named after the Native American wife of an early Montana settler. WAYNE MUMFORD

LEFT: Called "breaks," these broken hills rise above the Judith River near Winifred. JOHN LAMBING

PRECEDING PAGES: Lupine flowers paint swaths of purple in the Big Hole Valley. WAYNE MUMFORD

ABOVE: Ninepipes National Wildlife Refuge in the Mission Valley near Ronan protects more than 200 species of birds. WAYNE MUMFORD

FACING PAGE: Fall color glows on the banks of the North Fork of the Blackfoot River in Lolo National Forest. JOHN LAMBING

ABOVE: Unique metal sculpture found near East Glacier on the Blackfeet Indian Reservation. WAYNE MUMFORD

LEFT: The formations of the White Cliffs of the Missouri River near Fort Benton have fascinated and thrilled explorers since Lewis and Clark passed through here in the early 1800s. JOHN LAMBING

ABOVE: Historic church and school in Danvers stand the test of time. JOHN LAMBING

FACING PAGE: Mount Jackson overlooks Preston Park in Glacier's Siyeh Creek Basin. JOHN LAMBING

ABOVE: Glacier National Park patrol cabin surrounded by the archetypal jagged, snow-covered peaks of the park. WAYNE MUMFORD

FACING PAGE: The foothills of the Wolf Mountains on the Crow Reservation stretch toward the taller Bighorn Mountains in Wyoming. JOHN LAMBING

ABOVE: Still and silent, a great gray owl surveys its territory. WAYNE MUMFORD

LEFT: The Jefferson, Madison, and Gallatin Rivers combine to form the Missouri River at Missouri Headwaters State Park. WAYNE MUMFORD

ABOVE: Weathered barn near Bozeman. JOHN LAMBING

FACING PAGE: One of the most-photographed peaks in Glacier: Reynolds Mountain at Logan Pass. WAYNE MUMFORD

ABOVE: The bitterroot is Montana's state flower; these pink specimens bloom in the Big Hole Valley. WAYNE MUMFORD

RIGHT: The Tobacco Root Range overlooks the Jefferson River Valley near Twin Bridges. WAYNE MUMFORD

ABOVE: A family sleigh ride at Whitefish. WAYNE MUMFORD

FACING PAGE: Moonrise above a winter scene in Glacier National Park. WAYNE MUMFORD

ABOVE: White-tailed deer roam throughout Montana. WAYNE MUMFORD

RIGHT: Closeup view of an old-fashioned barn near Rock Creek. WAYNE MUMFORD

ABOVE: Fly fishing Blacktail Deer Creek near Dillon. WAYNE MUMFORD

LEFT: Wintry shadows chill the Tobacco Root Range near Pony. WAYNE MUMFORD

ABOVE: Built in 1898, Deer Lodge County Courthouse in Anaconda features a rotunda and copper-plated cupola. WAYNE MUMFORD

RIGHT: Hints of autumn along the Swan River near Bigfork. WAYNE MUMFORD

ABOVE: Preserved livery stable and wagons at Nevada City ghost town. JOHN LAMBING

FACING PAGE: Sun and shadow on Jerusalem Rocks near Sweetgrass on the Canadian border. JOHN LAMBING

ABOVE: A brave kayaker navigates Montana whitewater. WAYNE MUMFORD

RIGHT: Beautifully blue Georgetown Lake shimmers beneath the Anaconda Mountains. JOHN LAMBING

ABOVE: Religious icons at St. Ignatius Mission, one of the oldest buildings in the state. WAYNE MUMFORD

LEFT: A rare Montana wetland, Pine Butte Preserve serves as habitat for grizzly bears and other wildlife. WAYNE MUMFORD

ABOVE: A truly cavernous room inside the cave at Lewis and Clark Caverns State Park. WAYNE MUMFORD

RIGHT: Old wooden grain elevator at Ware in Fergus County. JOHN LAMBING

ABOVE: Charming small church in Lennep, a tiny burg near White Sulphur Springs. John Lambing

FACING PAGE: Fishing the Bitterroot River near Missoula on an autumn afternoon. John Lambing

ABOVE: Bronc-riding at the Helmville Labor Day Rodeo, called the "biggest little rodeo in Montana." Wayne Mumford

RIGHT: Winter sunrise along the North Fork of the Blackfoot River.
John Lambing

ABOVE: Quintessential Montana space: The Pines Recreation Area section of the Charles M. Russell National Wildlife Refuge, with Fort Peck Lake in the distance. WAYNE MUMFORD

LEFT: Recent rain has "greened up" the Missouri River Valley near Culbertson. JOHN LAMBING

ABOVE: Montana has seven American Indian reservations within the state borders. WAYNE MUMFORD

FACING PAGE: Golden morning light on the Tongue River near Ashland. JOHN LAMBING

ABOVE: Sport and relaxation near Creston. WAYNE MUMFORD

LEFT: A mile-high scene in the Anaconda-Pintler Wilderness. WAYNE MUMFORD

ABOVE: Evening light and shadow in the Flathead Valley. Wayne Mumford

FACING PAGE: Badger Creek courses along the Rocky Mountain Front on the Blackfeet Indian Reservation near Heart Butte. John Lambing

ABOVE: Virginia Falls is a popular hiking destination not far from
Going-to-the-Sun Road in Glacier National Park. WAYNE MUMFORD

FACING PAGE: Limestone cliffs and a natural window in the Gates
of the Mountains Canyon. JOHN LAMBING

FACING PAGE: Standing since the 1860s, Meade Hotel is now protected as part of Bannack State Park. WAYNE MUMFORD

LEFT: A moment in time at Garnet ghost town. WAYNE MUMFORD

BELOW: After a snowstorm in the Crazy Mountains near Wilsall. JOHN LAMBING

ABOVE: The Clark Fork near Alberton changes from a rushing torrent during spring runoff to a gently flowing waterway in the fall. JOHN LAMBING

FACING PAGE: Gunsight Lake and the border peaks of the St. Mary Valley in Glacier National Park. JOHN LAMBING

ABOVE: Cabin along Flint Creek in the western part of the state.
WAYNE MUMFORD

LEFT: Yellowstone River winds past badlands near Terry.
JOHN LAMBING

Above: Black Butte is a prominent feature of the Gravelly Range in Madison County.

John Lambing

Facing page: One of the last major undammed falls in the Northwest, Kootenai Falls near Libby is sacred to the Kootenai tribe, who continue to protect this scenic treasure.

John Lambing

ABOVE: A badger is camouflaged in a dry Montana meadow. JOHN LAMBING

RIGHT: Snow sticks around well into spring in the high country around West Yellowstone. WAYNE MUMFORD

ABOVE: Deadwood Falls swirls and bounces between the rocky cliffs along Reynolds Creek in Glacier National Park. JOHN LAMBING

FACING PAGE: Sunrise over Upsata Lake near Ovando. JOHN LAMBING

ABOVE: Remembering ranching heydays near Hilger. WAYNE MUMFORD

FACING PAGE: Autumn color at the base of sandstone cliffs near Colstrip. JOHN LAMBING

ABOVE: A surging natural spring, Giant Springs lies alongside the Missouri River in Great Falls. WAYNE MUMFORD

FACING PAGE: The granite peaks of the Pioneer Mountains surround pine forests, tranquil lakes, and mining ghost towns. JOHN LAMBING

ABOVE: Cattle check out an old homestead cabin in the foothills below the Big Snowy Mountains. JOHN LAMBING

LEFT: The Beaverhead River begins south of Dillon at Clark Canyon Reservoir, which has 17 miles of shoreline and offers good trout fishing. JOHN LAMBING

PRECEDING PAGES: The majestic Rocky Mountains rise from the Plains near Dupuyer. WAYNE MUMFORD

ABOVE: Pioneer wagon in a field near Whitehall. JOHN LAMBING

FACING PAGE: Sandstone formations below Miles Butte in the
Bears Paw Mountains south of Chinook. JOHN LAMBING

ABOVE: In the Flathead Valley the combining continues despite an approaching storm.
WAYNE MUMFORD

LEFT: Wildflowers on the prairie at Ear Mountain Wildlife Management Area.
JOHN LAMBING

115

ABOVE: Tenderfoot Creek flows through a canyon in the Lewis and Clark National Forest.
JOHN LAMBING

FACING PAGE: A lake on the Blackfeet Indian Reservation reflects Feather Woman Mountain,
which reaches skyward along the Rocky Mountain Front. JOHN LAMBING

ABOVE: A borate bomber fights a summer wildfire. WAYNE MUMFORD

RIGHT: This unique and beautiful scene is protected as part of the Upper Missouri River National Monument. WAYNE MUMFORD

NEXT PAGE: A new day dawns over Lake Sutherlin near White Sulphur Springs. JOHN LAMBING